Marvel's The Avengers

Based on the Screenplay by Joss Whedon
Story by Zak Penn and Joss Whedon

Produced by Kevin Feige, p.g.a.
Directed by Joss Whedon

Level 2

Retold by Jocelyn Potter

Series Editors: Andy Hopkins and Jocelyn Potter

Pearson Education Limited

KAO Two

KAO Park, Harlow,

Essex, CM17 9NA, England

and Associated Companies throughout the world.

ISBN: 978-1-292-20568-7

This edition first published by Pearson Education Ltd 2018

7 9 10 8

Set in 9pt/14pt Xenois Slab Pro

Printed by China

SWTC/07

Published by Pearson Education Limited

For a complete list of the titles available in the Pearson English Readers series, visit
www.pearsonenglishreaders.com.
Alternatively, write to your local Pearson Education office or
to Pearson English Readers Marketing Department,
Pearson Education, KAO Two, KAO Park, Harlow, Essex, CM17 9NA

Contents

Who's Who?

Tony Stark / Iron Man

He was a young man when his parents died. He is now head of his father's company, Stark Industries. He is very rich—and very smart. He built Iron Man's armor. It is a weapon, and protects him from attacks.

Steve Rogers / Captain America

He fought for his country, then almost died in the ocean. After 70 years under ice, he woke up. He is an Avenger now, but today's world is strange for him. His weapon is his powerful shield.

Bruce Banner / Hulk

He is another very smart man and one of the first Avengers. When Banner gets angry, he changes into the Hulk. The Hulk is very large, fast, strong, and dangerous.

Natasha Romanoff / Black Widow

She was an agent for the Soviet K.G.B. She attacked the U.S. and fought the Avengers. But now she lives in the U.S. and fights for the Avengers. She is strong and powerful.

S.H.I.E.L.D.

S.H.I.E.L.D is an American agency. It protects the country from attack. Nick Fury is the head of S.H.I.E.L.D. and gives the Avengers their jobs. Agent Phil Coulson often works with him.

Clint Barton / Hawkeye

He was one of S.H.I.E.L.D.'s best agents, a fighter and a thinker. Now he works with the Avengers. Nobody can use a bow and arrow better than he can.

Thor

When his father sent him away from his home in Asgard, he lost his great power. After he helped his new friends on Earth, his hammer—and his power—came back to him. Now he often works with the Avengers, and helps to protect Earth.

Loki

He is a tall, strong Asgardian. Thor's father killed his father and took Loki into his home. Everybody thinks that Thor is better than his brother Loki. That makes Loki angry. Now he has a scepter with great powers.

The Chitauri

The Chitauri are very strong, powerful, and dangerous. Their power comes from a Mother Ship. They—and The Other—work for Thanos. Thanos wants the powerful Tesseract.

The Avengers

Introduction

"You want to use the Avengers?" a man from S.H.I.E.L.D. asked. "You know that they're dangerous."

"They're strange—maybe crazy," Fury said. "But I think that they're our only hope."

Agent Nick Fury is talking about a very difficult and dangerous job. The U.S. agency S.H.I.E.L.D. had the Tesseract on Earth and wanted to use its great power. But Loki—an angry fighter from Asgard—took the Tesseract. He is also planning to attack Earth.

Who can protect Earth? Who can save its people and its cities? Who can find the Tesseract and take it from Loki? For Nick Fury, there is only one answer: the Avengers. They are all great fighters, but with very different powers. Will they help? He doesn't know. And before he can ask them, he has to find them.

Marvel's The Avengers is a 2012 movie with many great people in it. Robert Downey Jr. is Iron Man, Chris Evans is Captain America, Mark Ruffalo is the Hulk, Scarlett Johansson is the Black Widow, Jeremy Renner is Hawkeye, Chris Hemsworth is Thor, Tom Hiddleston is Loki, and Samuel Jackson is Agent Fury.

People around the world loved the movie. *Avengers: Age of Ultron* followed in 2015, and *Avengers: Infinity War* in 2018.

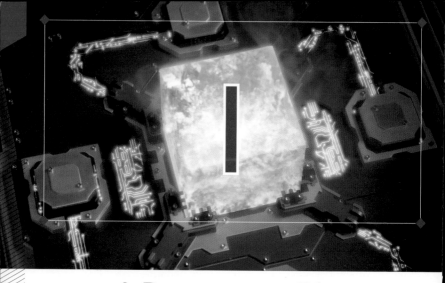

A Dangerous Plan

In a world a very long way from Earth, Loki stood in front of the Other. The Other looked into his eyes and spoke.

"The Tesseract is waking up," he said. "It is in a *little* world—the world of men. They want to use its power, but we have plans for it. Your job is this. Take it from them and bring it here to us."

"And why will I do that for you?" Loki asked.

"Because *we* helped *you*. You were angry when your brother Thor threw you out of your home on Asgard. We taught you many things, and we gave you your power—the scepter in your hand."

"Of course I was angry," Loki shouted. "*I* wanted Asgard, but Thor took it from me."

"Forget Asgard," the Other said. "You can have Earth—and with the Tesseract, my people can take many other, greater worlds."

"But first," Loki said, "your Chitauri spaceships have to help *me* take Earth. I will open the portal through space from the Tesseract for them. With your help, I will fight and win. When Earth is mine ... *then* I will bring you the Tesseract."

"Bring it to us," the Other said slowly, "or be very afraid."

The Power of the Tesseract

"Everybody out! Leave the building now and get away!"

People started to run outside. In the streets around the large building, they jumped into their cars and drove away as fast as possible.

"How bad is it?" Agent Fury shouted to Coulson, another agent.

The two men worked for S.H.I.E.L.D.

In a room below that building, S.H.I.E.L.D. protected the Tesseract. The agency had important plans for the Tesseract's great power, but now there was a problem.

"We don't know, sir," Coulson answered.

"What does Selvig say?" Fury asked.

"Dr. Selvig wasn't in the room when the Tesseract came on. We're not doing any tests on the machine, so he doesn't understand it. The Tesseract's power is getting stronger all the time. It's very dangerous, so we got the workers out."

Fury found Selvig. The doctor understood the Tesseract better than anybody.

"Talk to me, Selvig. What's happening?" Fury shouted.

"The Tesseract came on, sir, and I can't stop it," Selvig answered. "When I turn it off, it comes on again. I can't do anything with it."

"Where's Agent Barton?" Fury asked. Barton came and talked with him. "What's the problem here, Barton?" Fury asked. "Did you see anybody near the Tesseract?"

"Nobody went near it," Barton told him. "The problem's not here on Earth. It's at the other end."

"The other end?"

"Yes. You know that the Tesseract's a portal—a doorway to the other end of space. The door's now open at the other end. Somebody—or something—is coming down!"

The Tesseract made strange noises. The agents watched and waited.

Suddenly, there was an explosion of blue light. When the explosion ended, a tall man stood in front of them with a scepter in his hand. It was Loki.

Loki smiled, and it was not a pretty smile.

"Sir, please put down your weapon!" Fury called.

Loki looked down at his scepter. Then he looked up again and laughed. He ran at the agents. Their guns couldn't hurt Loki and he quickly killed many of them with his scepter.

Agent Barton was down. Loki ran to him and touched him with the end of his scepter. Barton's eyes slowly turned blue. Now Barton was Loki's man.

Fury watched. Without Barton, they had a problem. "I have to get the Tesseract out of here," he thought.

Quickly, he took the Tesseract from its big machine and put it in a small box. Then he moved away.

"Stop!" Loki said. "I want that, and I came a long way for it. I am Loki, of Asgard ..."

Selvig knew the name. "Loki, brother of Thor!" he said.

"We have no fight with your people," Fury said to Loki.

"Fight? Do you think that I'm afraid of *you*?" Loki said. "I'm going to take this world and make it mine. Make it easy for me and there will be no fighting."

He turned suddenly to Selvig and touched him with his scepter. Now Barton *and* Selvig worked for Loki.

There was thick blue smoke everywhere.

"We have to leave, sir," Barton told Loki. "This place is going to explode. Fury wants us to stay here and talk. Then we'll all die."

"I am Loki, of Asgard ..."

Selvig looked at the machine. "Barton's right," he said. "We have about two minutes."

Barton shot Fury and took the box with the Tesseract in it. He gave it to Selvig. Then he, Selvig, and Loki walked quickly out of the building to the agency cars.

But Fury wasn't dead. He used his radio and spoke to another agent, Agent Hill.

"Barton's with Loki," he shouted to the woman. "And Selvig, too. Stop them!"

Hill took out her gun, but Barton was faster. He shot, but didn't hit her. He and Selvig drove away, with Loki in the back. Hill shot at them but couldn't stop them.

Fury slowly stood up. One arm hurt badly, but he used his radio with his other hand.

"They have the Tesseract!" he shouted, and he ran outside.

Agent Hill jumped into a car and drove after Loki. Other agents followed. They shot at Loki, but he destroyed most of their cars with his scepter.

There was a big explosion and the S.H.I.E.L.D. building began to fall. Fury looked back unhappily. He called Hill again.

"We *have* to get that box," Fury told her. "Tell everybody. We can't lose the Tesseract."

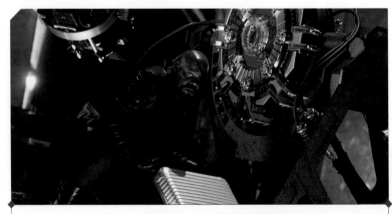

Quickly, Fury took the Tesseract from its big machine.

Call the Avengers!

Natasha Romanoff was in the hands of a Russian agency. The agents were not friendly.

"Who are you working for?" one asked angrily, in Russian. He hit her across the face. "Tell us now!"

A second agent answered his telephone, then gave it to his boss. "Strange," he said. "It's for her!"

"What?!" said the first agent. "Listen ..." he shouted into the phone.

An American spoke. "You're on the third floor of the Silensky Building," he said quietly, "and we have a fighter plane ten kilometers away from you. We can destroy the building before you can leave it. Now give the phone to the woman."

The agent gave Natasha the phone.

"We want you here," the American told her. "We have a problem with Barton."

Natasha quickly put down the phone. She jumped up and fought the two Russian agents. Then she left the building, with the phone.

"Bring Banner with you," the American said. "He's in India. Find him."

"Please help my family," a young Indian girl said to Bruce Banner. "People tell me that you're a doctor."

Banner followed the girl through the dark streets of the Indian city and into a small room. He stopped when he saw Natasha. So nobody was sick.

"You wanted a quiet, easy life?" Natasha said. "This is a strange place for that."

"Who are you?" Banner said quietly. "Who sent you?"

"I'm Natasha Romanoff. I'm here for S.H.I.E.L.D."

"S.H.I.E.L.D.! How did they find me?"

"They never lost you, Doctor, and they want your help again." She showed Bruce a picture on her phone. "This is the Tesseract," she said. "It can destroy us all. Somebody took it and Nick Fury wants you to find it."

"So he doesn't want Hulk?" Banner asked. "Fury knows that I can't be Hulk again. I *can't* get angry."

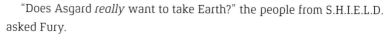

"Does Asgard *really* want to take Earth?" the people from S.H.I.E.L.D. asked Fury.

"Not Asgard," Fury said. "Only Loki. His brother Thor's our friend and protector. But Thor's a long way away. He can't help us."

"And you want to use the Avengers?" a man from S.H.I.E.L.D. asked. "You know that they're dangerous."

"They're strange—maybe crazy," Fury said. "But I think that they're our only hope."

Fury found Steve Rogers in his home town. "You look tired," he said.

"I slept for seventy years under the ocean, in the ice," Rogers answered. "I'm not tired. Are you here with a job for me, sir?"

"I am. Help us save the world." Fury gave Rogers a picture of the Tesseract. "Stark found that in the ocean when we found *you*. It's the answer to the world's energy problems. It will give us free energy—as much as we want. Can *you* tell us anything about the Tesseract?"

"The ocean was the best place for it. Who took it from you?"

"His name's Loki. He's not from this world. Are you with us?"

"It's time," Iron Man told his girlfriend on his radio. He flew high above the center of Manhattan in his armor. "Light up the building—now!"

Lights came on inside and outside the building. Iron Man could see the big blue letters of his name: STARK.

"Now we can tell people about our clean energy," Iron Man said. "This will *show* them—and everybody can have it."

Coulson showed Iron Man pictures of the Tesseract.

He flew to the Stark Building and went inside.

When Agent Coulson arrived from S.H.I.E.L.D., Iron Man wasn't interested. He was only interested in his energy.

"Please look at these." Coulson showed Iron Man pictures of the Tesseract.

"Are you bringing back the Avengers?" Iron Man asked.

Small planes arrived on a large ship. They carried Natasha Romanoff and Steve Rogers.

"It was exciting when they found you in the ocean," Natasha told Rogers. "Captain America wasn't dead!"

Another plane arrived.

"Dr. Banner!" Rogers called to Banner. "They say that you're a smart man. You can find the Tesseract."

"Hi, Rogers," Banner said. "I heard about you. This has to be strange for you, after years asleep under the ice."

"We have to go inside now," Natasha told them.

"Is this ship going underwater?" Rogers asked. "I can't do that again." But the ship climbed slowly up out of the ocean and flew.

"Doctor, thank you for coming," Agent Fury said to Banner.

"How long am I staying?" Banner asked.

"When we have the Tesseract, you can leave."

"Then show me my office," Banner said, "and I'll start looking. With the right machines and cameras, I'll find it."

In an underground room a long way away, Dr. Selvig was also at work. Loki and Clint Barton watched him with the Tesseract.

"Do you want anything?" Loki asked. "Tell me, and I'll get it."

"Yes, iridium. There is little of it on Earth, but maybe you can find some. It will make the Tesseract stronger and give it more power."

"We found Loki!" shouted one of Banner's helpers on the S.H.I.E.L.D. ship. "He's in Stuttgart, Germany."

"He wants iridium!" Banner said. "He knows that Heinrich Schafer has some there."

"Rogers," Agent Fury said, "this job's for you."

At a big party in Stuttgart, music played. Inside, people in fine clothes laughed and talked. Loki attacked Schafer. At the same time, Hawkeye—Clint Barton—killed people with his bow and arrow, then took the iridium from below the building.

Outside, Loki used his scepter and destroyed everything in his way. Then Loki shouted at the people in the street.

"Get down on the ground!" he said. They went down, afraid. "You think that you want to be free. But you don't. *Somebody* has to have power over you. Why not me?"

Then Loki shouted at the people in the street.

An older man stood up slowly. "Not *you*," he said. "I lived under Adolf Hitler. *You* will never have power over *me*."

"Really?" Loki laughed. Then he showed the man his scepter. "Watch," he said.

But before he could kill the old man, Captain America arrived. He flew down and saved the old man. Then he stood in front of Loki.

"I remember Hitler, too," he said. "He *also* enjoyed power over other people. It didn't go well for him."

"You're a man from the past," Loki laughed. "I'm not going to listen to you."

Above them, Black Widow arrived in a small plane. "Loki, put down your weapon!" she called.

Loki shot at the plane with his scepter, but Captain America attacked him. He and Loki fought, but Loki was stronger.

Then Iron Man flew down and ended the fight. Loki put his hands up.

Black Widow flew them all away from Stuttgart. Loki sat in the back of the plane and didn't speak.

"Was that a little easy?" Captain America asked.

Suddenly, the weather changed. There were lights in the dark sky. *THUD!* Somebody was on top of the plane!

It was Loki's brother, Thor. He flew inside and carried Loki out into the sky.

"What shall we do?" Captain America shouted.

"Attack!" Iron Man answered.

He flew outside, and Captain America followed.

Thor took Loki down to the ground.

"Where's the Tesseract?" he asked angrily. "Everybody in Asgard thinks that you're dead."

"Dead? Were you sad … *brother*?" Loki asked.

"We *were* brothers," Thor said. "We played, we fought …"

"But our father wasn't really my father—only yours. So now *you* have *my* country, Asgard."

"And you want Earth," Thor said. "No! *I* protect Earth."

"You're not doing a very good job!" Loki laughed. "Earth will be mine.

"We *were* brothers," Thor said. "We played, we fought ..."

I found a teacher and I learned a lot from him. He told me about the Tesseract. Its power will be mine, too."

"Who was your teacher?" Thor shouted. "The power of the Tesseract is very, very dangerous. Stop this now. Come home."

"I don't have the Tesseract," Loki said, "and you can't take me home without it. We have to leave through a portal."

Iron Man arrived. "Give Loki to me!" he told Thor.

"No," Thor said. "He has to answer questions—in Asgard."

"We want the Tesseract," Iron Man said. "When we have that, you can have Loki."

Thor threw his hammer and Iron Man fell to the ground. They fought on the ground and they fought in the sky. Thor attacked again and again with his hammer.

"Stop!" shouted Captain America at the two of them. "What are you doing?" he asked Thor.

"I have to stop Loki. He's dangerous," Thor said.

"So why are you fighting *us*?" Captain America said.

Thor thought about it. "You're right. Let's go," he said.

Thor and the two Avengers took Loki to S.H.I.E.L.D.'s ship. There, Fury put Loki in a big box of unbreakable glass.

"Don't try to get out," he said. "The floor will open, and it's a long way down through space to the ground."

"You didn't build this box for me," Loki smiled. "You built it for Hulk. He's working for you, but you're afraid of him."

Bruce Banner heard Loki's words. He never wanted to be Hulk again— but yes, a glass box had to be very strong for Hulk.

"You don't understand the power of the Tesseract," Fury told Loki. "I want to protect my world. Yes, we're afraid of Hulk, but we're more afraid of *you*. Now *you* can be afraid."

"You're angry because you *almost* had the power of the Tesseract," Loki laughed. "But *I* have it. The power is mine now."

Fury turned and walked away.

Dangerous Times

"Loki has fighters—the Chitauri," Thor told three of the Avengers. "He's going to attack Earth with them. Then, I think, he'll have to give the Tesseract to the Chitauri."

"So first, Loki has to build another portal from the Tesseract—with Dr. Selvig's help," Banner said. "The Chitauri will come from space through that portal."

"With Selvig's help? Selvig's a friend," Thor said.

"Not now. Loki touched him with his scepter and he now has power over him—and over Barton," Natasha told him.

"Loki's fighters are coming from space," Rogers said. "So why is he on this ship? How did we catch him so easily? I think he has a plan."

"Loki and Barton took the iridium in Stuttgart for the Tesseract," Banner said.

"Yes, remember the explosion in the S.H.I.E.L.D. building?" Stark told Rogers. "Iridium will stop that happening. Also, the new portal will stay open—wide open—for as long as Loki wants. But before he can start the Tesseract, he has to find a place with power for it—a *lot* of power."

Stark started working with Banner in a room full of computers. They had to know everything about the Tesseract.

"Come to the Stark Building one day," Stark said. "I have a lot of machines. You can play with them."

"Thank you," Banner answered. "But when I was in New York before, I destroyed Harlem."

"I won't make you angry," Stark said. Then he hit Banner.

"Hey!" Banner shouted—but Hulk stayed inside him.

"Good!" Stark laughed.

Rogers saw them. "That was a really bad idea, Stark," he said. "And why aren't you working?"

"I am," Stark said. "But I'm also thinking: Why did Fury call us *now*? Why not earlier? What isn't he telling us?"

"No idea." Rogers said. He turned to Banner. "What do you think about Loki's plans?" he asked.

"I think that he's interested in the Stark Building," Banner said slowly. "Barton told him about it—or he heard about it. Everybody's talking about Stark's new, clean energy. Loki can use that power for the Tesseract."

"So why didn't S.H.I.E.L.D. call you when they *found* the Tesseract?" Banner asked Stark. "You know about power and they didn't use you. And why *is* S.H.I.E.L.D. interested in energy? That's not its job."

"I'm working on an answer to that," Stark said. "My computer's trying to break into S.H.I.E.L.D.'s."

"What?!" Rogers said angrily. "You can't do that. We have to protect the Earth. *That's* our job. So find the Tesseract!"

He left the room—but he started to look around the ship. *Did* the Avengers know everything about S.H.I.E.L.D.'s plans?

"What does Loki plan for Dr. Selvig after this?" Thor asked Agent Coulson. "Erik Selvig's a good man."

"He often talks about you," Coulson said. "Everything changed on

Earth after you started to protect us."

"I do my best—but did we Asgardians destroy more than we helped?" Thor asked. "When I first came here, Loki followed me. He was angry, and many of your people died. And now it's happening again."

Fury came into the room. "Where does Loki have the Tesseract?" he asked Thor. "Will he tell you?"

"No—he's angry with me," Thor answered. "I can hurt him, but he won't talk. What's the problem? He can't leave here."

"So why do I think that Loki *wants* to be here?" Fury asked.

Natasha stood in front of the glass box.

"Do they want me to think that you're my friend?" Loki asked. "Did they send you for some answers?"

"What did you do to Agent Barton?" Natasha asked. "And what will you do when he finishes his work for you?"

"Ah, Barton. Is this love, Agent Romanoff?"

"Love is for children," Natasha answered. "Before I worked for S.H.I.E.L.D., I worked for some very bad people. S.H.I.E.L.D. sent Barton after me. But he didn't kill me—he saved me. Now *I* have to help *him*."

"Your world is near its end and you want to save one man!" Loki smiled. "I have a plan for the two of you. First, I'll tell Barton to kill you. Then I'll turn him into an agent again so he can see his work. When he cries, I'll kill *him*."

"What *are* you?" Natasha shouted angrily.

"What am *I*?" Loki said. "You brought something worse—much, much worse—than me onto this ship."

Natasha smiled. Suddenly, she understood. "So that's your plan," she said. "You want to use Hulk!" She spoke into her radio. "Fury," she said, "Banner can't go near Loki."

"What did you do to Agent Barton?" Natasha asked.

"What are you doing?" Fury asked Stark and Banner. "Aren't you looking for the Tesseract?"

"Our computers are," Stark said. "We'll find it. But what's next, Fury? What does S.H.I.E.L.D. really want?" He turned a computer around and showed Fury plans for a missile. "We know now. It has another use for the Tesseract's power—for weapons."

"Did you know about this?" Banner asked Fury angrily.

Natasha and Thor walked in.

"Are you getting angry, Banner?" Natasha asked unhappily. "Loki *wants* you angry. Do you want to leave the ship?"

"No, I'm not leaving," Banner said. He turned back to Fury. "Why is S.H.I.E.L.D. using the Tesseract for weapons?"

"Because of Thor," Fury said.

"Me?" Thor said.

"Last year, your people came here from space and destroyed a small town. Now we know that we're not the only world. We also know that people from other worlds have more powerful weapons."

"Asgard won't attack you again," Thor said.

"But you're not the only fighters out there."

"Loki's here this time because you started working with the Tesseract," Thor said angrily. "Now his friends want it. They know that you're making better weapons. Now *they* want better weapons, too. How does it end?"

"But S.H.I.E.L.D. has to protect Earth," Natasha told the other Avengers. "It *has* to have the best weapons."

Everybody was angry now.

"Natasha, please take Banner back to his room," Fury said.

"Which room? You gave *my* room to Loki," Banner shouted. "When Hulk comes out, you want to put *him* in there. Then you want to kill him. But you can't kill Hulk. I know. I tried. I was a good man in India. I helped people. Why did you bring me here?"

Loki's scepter was on the table behind him. Then, suddenly, it was in Banner's hand.

"Dr. Banner," Rogers said quietly. "Put down the scepter."

A sound came from one of the computers.

"The Tesseract!" Banner said. He put down the scepter. "We found it." But his eyes stayed on the computer. "Oh, no!" he said—and then something hit the ship.

There was a loud explosion, and then a fire.

"There's a problem with the ship!" Agent Hill shouted. "Barton's here, with Loki's men."

"Get us over water before the ship falls," Fury shouted into his radio. "Stark and Rogers, go outside and look at the problem. Coulson, don't take your eyes off Loki!"

After the explosion, Natasha and Banner were on the floor.

"We're O.K.," Natasha told Banner. Then she saw a change in him. "Bruce? What's happening?" She was afraid now. "This is Loki's plan. Don't get angry. You can walk away …"

But Banner changed into something bigger—and stronger—and uglier. He turned green. Hulk was born again!

Hulk looked angrily at Natasha. Then he made a loud noise and she ran. In his glass box, Loki heard the sound of Hulk and smiled.

Natasha ran, but Hulk was faster. Before he could kill her, Thor saved her. Then Thor fought Hulk. But Hulk was bigger, stronger, and very dangerous.

"We're your friends, Banner!" Thor shouted. "Stop!"

Hulk threw him across the room.

Thor called for his hammer and they fought again. Now Thor was stronger—now Hulk.

Agent Hill had an idea. She used her radio and called an agent in a small plane. "Fly near our ship and shoot at Hulk!" she said.

The agent shot through the window and Hulk fell. But then he stood up, angrier than before. He jumped out of the window onto the plane. He pulled the top off it and threw the agent out. Then Hulk fell, too.

Hulk jumped out of the window onto the plane.

Black Widow listened to her radio. "Barton's on our ship with Loki's men," she heard. "He destroyed some of the computers and now he's on his way to Loki. Can anybody stop him?"

"I can," she answered.

Barton was Hawkeye now. She found him and attacked him. Hawkeye caught her—then took out a knife. She pushed him away, hard. He fell and hit his head.

"Natasha?" he said slowly. Was this a different Hawkeye?

She hit him across the face.

Thor arrived at the glass box and found Loki at the open door.

"No!" he shouted.

He ran at Loki with his hammer, but Loki was faster. Suddenly, Thor was in the glass box. Loki stood outside and touched the computer. The door to the box closed.

Angrily, Thor hit the glass with his hammer, but he couldn't break it.

"Earth people think that you and I can't die," Loki laughed, and turned to the computer again. "Let's see …"

But Agent Coulson stood in front of him, with a very powerful weapon.

"Do you like this?" Coulson said. "It's new. We started work on it after your *last* visit to Earth."

But again, Loki moved quickly. He pushed his scepter into the agent.

"No!" Thor cried again.

Loki went back to the computer and smiled at Thor. The floor below the glass box opened and the box fell away from the ship.

On the way down, Thor tried to break the glass with his hammer again and again. One more time … The glass broke and Thor jumped out. Then the box hit the ground.

On the ship, Coulson was weak now. "You're going to lose," he told Loki slowly.

Loki smiled. "Your ship is falling from the sky," he said. "Why do you think that *I'm* going to lose?"

He laughed and walked away.

Fury arrived and found Coulson on the floor.

"I'm sorry, boss," Agent Coulson said—and died.

The Avengers heard about Coulson on their radios. They all knew him well and were very sad.

Rogers and Stark saved the ship. But when the two men met with Fury, he was unhappy about the other problems.

"Loki's not on the ship now," he told them, "so we can't get the Tesseract. Banner and Thor aren't here. And yes, you were right—S.H.I.E.L.D. wanted to build missiles with the Tesseract. But *I* had *another* plan for the future—a plan for the Avengers. Each of you has powers. Without you—all of you—we can't win these big fights."

The End of the World?

On the ground, a long way below the ship, Thor looked for his hammer.

Also on the ground, but inside a building, Bruce Banner sat up, tired and dirty. He looked around and saw an older man.

"Did I destroy this building?" he asked. "Did I hurt anybody?"

"There's nobody here," the man said, "but the birds didn't like it."

"You saw me fall?"

"I did. You fell from the sky—big and green and with no clothes. Here—" The man threw some clothes to him. "They're your size now. They weren't when you arrived."

Banner quickly put on the clothes. "Thank you," he said.

"You're not from Earth?"

"Yes, I'm from here."

"Then you have a problem, son," the man said.

On the S.H.I.E.L.D. ship, Natasha sat with Barton. When Barton woke up, he didn't look well.

"Clint," Natasha said, "you're going to be all right."

"Loki was in my head. How did you get him out?"

"I hit you really hard."

"Thanks." Barton looked afraid. "How many agents did I kill?"

"Don't think about it."

"Did Loki get away?"

"Yes. Where is he? Do you know?"

"No. I didn't ask." Barton stood up. "But he's going to use the Tesseract today. He's ready."

"We have to stop him."

"I'd like to put an arrow in his eye," Barton said. "But why are *you* in this fight, Natasha?"

"I'm an Avenger now. I want to do some good."

"I don't like working for Fury," Stark told Rogers. "He and Loki aren't very different."

"No," Rogers said. "But we have to forget that and do this job. Let's think. Loki has to have energy for the Tesseract."

"Yes, and he wants people to *see* him win. He wants a building with his name on it …" Stark stopped and thought. "Banner was right! The Stark Building!" He ran out of the room.

Rogers found Natasha. "We have to go," he said. "Can you fly one of the small planes?"

"*I* can," Barton said.

Rogers looked at him, then at Natasha.

"It's O.K.," she said. "Barton's with us now."

The Avengers walked to a plane.

Fury saw the plane leave. "I think they're going to Loki," he told Agent Hill. "We have to see this. Turn on cameras everywhere."

"Yes, sir."

Dr. Selvig placed his machines on top of the Stark Building. The Tesseract was ready. He watched and waited.

"Turn that off!" Iron Man shouted from above him.

"I can't!" Selvig said. "Nobody can stop it now."

Iron Man tried to attack it. Selvig fell, but the power of the Tesseract was greater than Iron Man's.

Loki watched and laughed. "The new portal is open," he said. "The Chitauri fighters are coming and nothing will change that. What do I have to be afraid of?"

Stark took off his armor. "The Avengers," he said. Loki looked at him. "That's our name. Earth's greatest fighters ..."

Loki laughed again. "I met them," he said.

"We're getting better at the job," Stark said. "But think about it. Your brother's with us. Also a very, *very* angry and dangerous man. We're all angry with *you*."

Loki smiled. "That was the plan. And the Chitauri are with me."

"We have Hulk. You can't win this. But maybe the Chitauri *are* stronger and more powerful than us. Maybe we *can't* protect the Earth. Then we'll *avenge* it."

"First your Avengers will have to fight *you* because you'll be *mine*," Loki said, and he touched Stark with his scepter.

Nothing happened. Stark laughed, and the two men began to fight. Loki was stronger, but Stark radioed for his armor.

Before the armor arrived, Loki pushed Stark through the glass window. It was a long way down, and people in the street looked up, afraid. But when Stark was almost at the ground, his armor flew out through the window, down, and around him.

Iron Man suddenly flew up again, into the sky.

"You made another person angry, too," he shouted at Loki. "This is for Phil Coulson."

He shot at Loki and Loki fell.

On top of the building, a blue light exploded from the Tesseract and shot high into the sky. A long way away, in space, the portal opened and Chitauri spaceships started to fly down to Earth.

Iron Man looked up.

"Oh, no! They're coming," he said, and flew up into the sky.

When the spaceships came out the other end, over the tall buildings of Manhattan, Iron Man fought them, one after the other. The spaceships caught fire and fell to the ground.

But Iron Man couldn't stop the spaceships coming. Many more flew down.

From the streets below, people saw the spaceships and the fires. Cars stopped. Their drivers got out and watched. Then, when spaceships hit their cars, they ran.

The Chitauri shot at people in the streets and killed them. They shot at cars and destroyed them. There were fires everywhere, outside and inside buildings.

Loki was on his feet again. With his scepter in his hand, he watched from the top of the Stark Building and smiled.

"Loki!" It was Thor. "Turn off the Tesseract or I'll destroy it."

Loki laughed. "You can't. And nobody can stop it now."

He jumped at Thor and they fought. Loki used his scepter and Thor used his hammer. They hit the STARK name on the outside of the building, and the *K* fell to the ground.

Police cars arrived in the streets below. Policemen jumped out and looked up at the Chitauri spaceships. Then they saw a small, fast plane.

"We're over the city," Black Widow said into the plane's radio.

"You're late!" Iron Man shouted. "Did you stop for lunch on the way? Fly over the park. I'll take them there."

Iron Man flew to the park and the spaceships followed. The plane followed the spaceships and shot some of them down.

"More are coming!" Iron Man heard on his radio.

"That's fine," he said. "We'll destroy them, too."

In the plane, Hawkeye and Black Widow flew past the Stark Building. They saw the fight between Loki and Thor.

Loki hit Thor hard. Then, when Hawkeye flew the plane near the building, Loki shot at it. Thor got up and hit Loki. They fought again.

But the plane was on fire and it started to fall. Hawkeye flew it down onto a street. Captain America, Hawkeye, and Black Widow jumped out and ran to the Stark Building.

On the way, they heard a very loud noise above them. They stopped and looked up. The portal was wide open now, and they could see many more Chitauri spaceships. One was very, very big. How many Chitauri fighters were in that?

When the big ship flew down, it destroyed everything in its way. The three Avengers watched. What could they do?

The Chitauri jumped out and onto the tall buildings. They broke through windows and used powerful guns on the people inside.

"Iron Man, do you see this?" Captain America shouted on his radio.

"Yes!" Iron Man answered. "Where's Banner? Is he here?"

"I don't know."

"Tell me when you find him."

Up on the Stark Building, Thor shouted at Loki. "Look around you! You're crazy. Do you think that the Chitauri will save this world for you? They're destroyers."

Loki looked afraid. "I can't stop this now," he said quietly.

"But *we* can," Thor said. "You and I." He took Loki's arms.

Suddenly, Loki pushed a knife into his brother. Thor's hammer fell and Thor fell, too.

"You're weak," Loki laughed. "You have *feelings*. You can't win."

He jumped from the top of the building onto one of the smaller Chitauri spaceships, and flew away. Thor pulled the knife out.

Down in the street, Captain America, Black Widow, and Hawkeye looked up at the Chitauri spaceships. They had to do something.

"People up here in this building can't get out," Iron Man called on his radio.

Loki flew past them, with Chitauri fighters around him.

The Chitauri shot at the streets. There were loud explosions around the Avengers and more cars and buildings caught fire. Policemen ran from the fires.

"The people in the street are going to die!" Captain America said. "We have to help."

"Hawkeye and I will do it," Black Widow told him. "Go and help Iron Man."

Captain America looked at Hawkeye.

"Can you stop these fighters?" he asked.

"I'll enjoy it," Hawkeye answered.

Hawkeye put an arrow in his bow and shot at a Chitauri fighter. The arrow went through the fighter's armor and he fell. Hawkeye turned quickly to the next fighter—and the next. Black Widow stood up with a gun in each hand and started to shoot, too. Some Chitauri died; others had to move away. People climbed out of buses and buildings, and ran.

With his shield in his hand, Captain America jumped from car to car. The Chitauri shot at him, but his shield protected him.

At the end of the street, policemen shot at the Chitauri from behind their cars.

Hawkeye put an arrow in his bow and shot at a Chitauri fighter.

"We can't kill all of them!" one policeman shouted to another man. "What can we do?"

Captain America stopped running and shouted to the policemen. "Send men into these buildings," he told them. "There are people inside. They're afraid and they're not going to wait there. They'll run outside into the street and get hurt. Take them into underground rooms or into the subway! Then get everybody out of this street and the streets near here."

"Who are you? I'm not going to listen to *you*!" one policeman said angrily.

A Chitauri fighter shot at Captain America and jumped on him. But Captain America turned and used his shield. Then he turned again and killed a second Chitauri ... and a third ... and a fourth.

The policeman watched, then turned to the other policemen.

"Take people underground, and away from these streets!" he shouted. "I want everybody out of these streets—now!"

Iron Man flew past the large spaceship. It turned and followed him.

"It's behind me!" he called on his radio. "Now what?!"

Hawkeye and Black Widow couldn't stop fighting Chitauri on the street. Captain America was with them again now, but they were all tired.

When the fighting stopped for a time, Thor arrived.

"What's happening with the Tesseract?" Captain America asked him. "Can we close the portal?"

"No, the Tesseract's power is very, very strong. We can't get near it," Thor said.

Iron Man flew past. "Thor's right," he called. "We can't stop fighting."

"But I want to get my hands on Loki," Thor said angrily.

"We *all* want to do that," Hawkeye said.

"Think about Loki later," Captain America told them. "He wants the Chitauri to attack us, and that's good. The fight will stay here, in Manhattan. But Iron Man's up there in the sky. We have to help him—"

He stopped and looked down the street. The other Avengers looked, too. Was that ...? Yes, it was Banner.

Banner looked around at the buildings and the cars. There were fires and glass and dead Chitauri everywhere.

"This doesn't look very nice," he said.

"There are worse things," Black Widow said quietly.

"Hulk? Yes, I'm sorry," Banner said.

"Don't be sorry. We can *use* something worse now," Black Widow said.

"Banner's here," Captain America told Iron Man on his radio.

"Good," Iron Man said. "I'm bringing the party to you."

He flew around a building into their street. The large Chitauri spaceship followed. It destroyed everything in its way.

"The 'party'!" Black Widow said.

"Dr. Banner," said Captain America. "Are you feeling angry? Now's a really, really good time."

"I never told anybody this," Banner said with a half-smile, "but I'm *always* angry."

He turned to the spaceship and got bigger, stronger, uglier—and green. Hulk was born again.

Hulk stopped the big spaceship with one hand. Iron Man shot at it, and the other Avengers had to turn away from the fire. Angry Chitauri climbed out of buildings around them and started to attack. But in the middle of the street, back to back, stood Thor, with his hammer in his hand, and the Avengers: big green Hulk, Iron Man in his armor, Captain America with his shield, Hawkeye with his bow and arrow, and Black Widow.

Loki looked down on them and spoke into a radio. "Send the other spaceships," he said.

More large Chitauri spaceships flew down through the portal.

"We have to close the portal," Captain America said, "but we can't do that now. We can only protect this city and the people in it. Barton, you go up on a high building. Watch everything and tell us. Stark, you go to the end of the street. When a spaceship tries to come in, stop it."

"Can you take me up?" Hawkeye asked Iron Man.

Iron Man put him under his arm and carried him up to the top of a building.

"Thor," Captain America said, "go up to the bottom of the portal. Stop as many spaceships as you can!"

Thor flew away.

"Good," Iron Man said. "I'm bringing the party to you."

Captain America turned to Black Widow. "You and I will stay and fight here," he said. "And Hulk—destroy!"

Hulk jumped up to the Chitauri fighters on the outside of the buildings. He killed one, then another, then another. He jumped across the street and didn't stop killing.

On top of the tallest building, Thor shot power into the sky from his hammer. Spaceships caught fire and fell.

Angry Chitauri climbed out of buildings around them and started to attack.

Do or Die

From the top of another building, Hawkeye used his bow and arrow.

"Stark," he called into his radio, "there are spaceships behind you."

"I know," Iron Man answered. "When they follow me, they stay away from the streets. I'll bring them to you."

He turned quickly and the spaceships turned with him. Hawkeye shot some of them down. Others flew into buildings and exploded.

"Nice!" Iron Man called. "Now what?"

"Help Thor. He's on the ground now and fighting a lot of Chitauri."

Hulk ran through an office building and out again. He jumped onto a big spaceship and pulled it down.

Black Widow fought hard, like a wild animal. She was tired when Captain America arrived.

"This will never end. We have to close that portal," she said.

"Our biggest guns can't destroy the Tesseract."

"It's not always about guns," she answered. "Help me up there."

She jumped onto Captain America's shield, and up onto a Chitauri spaceship. She killed the fighters on the ship, then flew it through the streets, on her way to the Stark Building.

More and more spaceships arrived, but the Avengers fought in the streets, on buildings, and in the sky.

Hulk helped Thor. They destroyed the largest ship and everybody on it.

On the Stark Building, Dr. Selvig woke up and looked around him. Where was he? What happened? He didn't understand.

"There are a lot of people in the bank on 42nd Street, and the Chitauri are in there with them!" Iron Man shouted into his radio.

"I'm on my way," Captain America answered.

He jumped in through the window of the bank and fought wildly. Some Chitauri died, but others ran at him.

"Leave now!" he shouted to the people in the bank.

They ran.

A Chitauri fighter had his arms around Captain America. He fought, but the Chitauri threw him out of a window. He hit a car, hard. How could he and the other Avengers end this? For the first time, Captain America felt afraid.

Up on the S.H.I.E.L.D. ship, Fury watched pictures of the streets of New York on the computers.

"Sir!" Agent Hill said. "S.H.I.E.L.D. wants to talk with you."

The pictures on the computers changed to the men and women of S.H.I.E.L.D.

"Agent Fury," a man said, "what happened? We didn't ask you—we *told* you. You have nuclear missiles on your ship. You have to use them and destroy Manhattan. We'll lose Manhattan, but save the world. It's the only way."

"I'm *not* going to send nuclear missiles into New York," Fury said angrily. "They'll kill tens of thousands of people. First, let's wait and see.

For the first time, Captain America felt afraid.

The Avengers are fighting hard. Maybe they can win."

"Maybe they can't," the man said. "Send the missiles or we'll lose everything."

"No!" Fury answered.

Loki followed Black Widow. When he shot at her, Hawkeye saw them from above. He shot at Loki, but Loki caught the arrow easily in one hand. Then he and Black Widow jumped from their spaceships down onto the Stark Building. Black Widow ran to the Tesseract.

Hulk arrived, too, and threw Loki through a window.

"Stop!" Loki shouted. Hulk stopped and looked at him. "I'm Loki, from Asgard. Are you crazy? You can't hurt me!"

Hulk attacked and hit him again and again—and again. "*I* can't hurt *you*?" he said, and he walked away.

He left Loki on the floor. Loki couldn't move.

Black Widow found Selvig. He was hurt, but he was a friend again now.

"The scepter …" Selvig said. "The Tesseract—I didn't tell anybody, but we *can* turn it off. With the energy from Loki's scepter, we can close the portal."

In the streets below, Thor destroyed spaceships with his hammer. Iron Man flew into a big ship and destroyed it with an explosion from inside. Hawkeye fought with his bow and arrows. Hulk didn't stop killing. But more and more Chitauri spaceships arrived through the portal.

S.H.I.E.L.D. didn't wait. They sent a plane with a nuclear missile without telling Fury. Fury saw it on his computer, and he could do nothing about it.

He called Iron Man on his radio. "Stark, do you hear me? There's a nuclear missile on its way to the city."

"What?! How long will it take?" Iron Man shouted.

"Three minutes." Fury told him. "It will destroy Manhattan."

Somewhere outside the city, the nuclear missile left the plane. Two and a half minutes …

Hulk didn't stop killing.

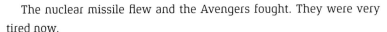

The nuclear missile flew and the Avengers fought. They were very tired now.

On the Stark Building, Black Widow found Loki's scepter and started to push it slowly, slowly into the Tesseract.

"I can close the portal," she shouted to the others through the radio.

"Do it!" Captain America answered.

"No, wait!" Iron Man called. "There's a nuclear missile on its way. We have under a minute before it arrives. I have to stop it. I can see it now …"

He flew to the missile and caught it in his arms. Then Iron Man flew with the missile over Manhattan, over the Stark Building, up, up into the portal.

New York was safe—but Iron Man wasn't.

Then Iron Man flew with the missile over Manhattan ..., up, up into the portal.

Inside the portal, he took his hands off the missile. It flew up, out of the other end of the portal, to the Chitauri mother ship, and exploded. In Manhattan, all the Chitauri spaceships fell to the ground and every fighter died.

The other Avengers looked up at the sky and waited. They couldn't see Iron Man. Was he dead?

Iron Man wasn't dead, but he had to get out of the portal. He couldn't fly, so he fell—down, down, down through the long portal.

"He's dead. We can't wait. Close the portal!" Captain America told Black Widow quietly through his radio.

"No, let's wait," Black Widow said. "Maybe he *isn't* dead."

"We *can't* wait," Captain America said sadly. "Do it!"

She pushed the scepter, with its great energy, into the Tesseract, and above her the portal slowly closed.

The Avengers all looked up. Was this the end of Iron Man?

Suddenly, they saw him. He was outside the portal and falling fast.

"Help him!" Thor shouted.

Hulk jumped from the top of a building and caught Iron Man in his arms. They hit the ground hard. Hulk stood up, but Iron Man didn't move.

Captain America and Thor ran to them. They all waited. Was Iron Man really dead? Then Hulk made a loud, ugly noise and Iron Man's eyes opened wide.

"What was *that*?" he said. "What happened?"

"We won," Captain America said quietly.

"Good," Iron Man said with a half-smile. "Let's take a vacation tomorrow. One day without work. What do you think?"

Thor looked unhappy. "We have another job first," he said.

Later, in the Stark Building, Loki slowly sat up. His head, his legs— everything hurt.

In front of him stood the Avengers and his brother. They didn't look friendly.

More Questions
than Answers

People in every American city, and in every country in the world, talked about the attack on Manhattan and about the Avengers. There were parties. Children fought spacemen in their games. Newspapers were full of the story. People talked about it on television:

"The attackers killed a lot of people and destroyed a lot of buildings. But the Avengers saved us!"

"We can sleep safely in our beds because the Avengers are protecting us."

"I love you, Thor!" a young woman shouted.

Not everybody was happy:

"What aren't they telling us about the attack?"

"Those people destroyed our city. Who's going to pay? It was *their* fight—and where are they now?"

But television also showed a young woman in a Manhattan street. She was tired and dirty, but she smiled.

"Captain America saved my life," she said. "I'd like to say thank you."

"Where *are* the Avengers?" one of the men from S.H.I.E.L.D. asked Fury.

"I don't know," he answered. "I don't *want* to know. They're on vacation."

"And the Tesseract?"

"The Tesseract is back in its right place—not in our hands."

"Loki?"

"Loki isn't our problem now," Fury said. "He won't come back."

In a park a long way from New York, Thor took Loki and the Tesseract from the Avengers. He opened a portal with the Tesseract, then he, Loki, and the Tesseract flew through it on their way to Asgard.

The Avengers watched. Then they said goodbye and went their different ways.

"You started something when you used the Avengers, Agent Fury," a woman from S.H.I.E.L.D. said angrily. "They're dangerous."

"Yes, they are," Fury said slowly. "And now the world knows that. *Every* world knows that."

He turned away from the computers, to Agent Hill.

"What happens now?" Hill asked. "They left, and some have lives a long way from here. What do we do when we want them again?"

"They'll come back," Fury said.

"Will they?"

"They will."

"Why?"

"Because we can't win our fights without them."

Activities

Chapters 1–2

Before you read

1   Look at the Word List at the back of the book. Discuss these questions.

  a What are the meanings of the words in your language?
  b What can you use when you want to hurt somebody?
  c What can help to protect you in a fight?

2   Read the Introduction to this story at the front of the book and answer these questions.

  a Why is the Tesseract important?
  b What is Loki going to do?
  c Why does Agent Fury want the help of the Avengers?
  d Why are the people from S.H.I.E.L.D. unhappy about the Avengers?

3   Turn to the Who's Who? pages at the front of the book and discuss these questions.

  a Look at the pictures. Which of these people do you know, from books or movies? What do you know about them?
  b Read the sentences below the pictures. Were you right? Did you learn anything new?

While you read

4   Circle the right words.

  a Loki has to take the *scepter / Tesseract* from Earth for the Other.
  b The Other will give Loki Chitauri spaceships for his attack on *Asgard / Earth*.
  c Nobody understands the Tesseract better than *Fury / Selvig*.
  d The Tesseract *comes on / goes off* because Loki is on his way down the portal.
  e After he touches them with his scepter, *Coulson / Barton* and Selvig work for Loki.
  f Loki leaves the S.H.I.E.L.D. building *without / with* the Tesseract.

After you read

5   Which of these people are working with S.H.I.E.L.D. now?

The Other   Agent Fury   Agent Coulson   Dr. Selvig
Agent Barton   Loki   Agent Hill

6   Work with another student. Have this conversation.

Student A: You are an important man or woman in S.H.I.E.L.D. Talk to Agent Fury. Where is he? What is happening? What is he going to do? How do you feel?

Student B: You are Nick Fury. Answer the questions. Tell the story and talk about your plans.

Chapters 3–4

Before you read

7   Discuss these questions. What do you think?

    a What is Fury going to do now?
    b What is Loki going to do?

While you read

8   Find the word *iridium* in your dictionary. What is it? What are its special qualities?

9   Who is speaking? Write the names.

    a "They never lost you, Doctor."   ....
    b "I can't be Hulk again."   ....
    c "I'm not tired."   ....
    d "Light up the building—now!"   ....
    e "Iridium will give the Tesseract more power."   ....
    f "Somebody has to have power over you."   ....
    g "I protect Earth."   ....
    h "Now you can be afraid."   ....

10 Finish the sentences.

    a The Chitauri will come through a .... to Earth.

b Loki has to find a place with a lot of .... for the Tesseract.

c S.H.I.E.L.D. wants to use the Tesseract for energy and ....

d When Barton arrives at the ship, there is a big ....

e Hulk falls to the ground, on Earth, from the top of a small
....

f Loki kills Coulson with his ....

g Thor jumps out of the glass .... before it hits the ground.

h Fury wants to use the Avengers'............................ in future fights, too.

After you read

11 Thor says, "They know that you're making better weapons. Now they want better weapons, too. How does it end?" Discuss these questions.

a What does Thor mean?

b What answer does Natasha give him?

c What do you think?

Chapter 5

Before you read

12 Fury and the Avengers now have a lot of problems. Write notes on them. Then show your notes to other students. Did you think of everything?

While you read

13 Who is talking? Who are these people talking about?

a "You fell from the sky."

....

b "I'd like to put an arrow in his eye."

....

c "That's our name. Earth's greatest fighters."

....

d "Oh, no! They're coming."

....

e "Look around you! You're crazy!"

....

f "You have feelings. You can't win."

....

g "Take them into underground rooms or into the subway!"

....

h "We can use something worse now."

....

After you read

14 Answer these questions.

    a Why isn't Banner wearing any clothes when he hits the ground?
    b How does Natasha bring Barton back to the Avengers?
    c Why do Loki and Selvig take the Tesseract to the Stark Building?
    d What happens when the Tesseract opens a new portal into space?
    e Why do the policemen listen to Captain America?
    f What can Hulk do, and not the other Avengers?

15 How do the Avengers fight the Chitauri and their spaceships? Discuss each Avenger with another student.

Chapters 6-7

Before you read

16 Discuss these questions.

    a How will the fight end?
    b What will New Yorkers think about the Avengers?
    c What will S.H.I.E.L.D. think about them?

While you read

17 Are these sentences right (✔) or wrong (✘)?

    a Powerful guns can destroy the Tesseract ◯
    b Selvig stops working for Loki. ◯
    c Fury wants to kill the Chitauri with nuclear weapons. ◯

d Loki's scepter can turn off the Tesseract. ◯
e Captain America saves Manhattan from the nuclear weapon. ◯
f Hulk wakes Iron Man up with a loud, ugly noise. ◯
g Americans are all happy with the Avengers' work. ◯
h S.H.I.E.L.D. has the Tesseract again. ◯

After you read

18 **Answer these questions.**

  a When Black Widow goes from the street to the Stark Building, how does she go there?
  b When a Chitauri fighter throws Captain America out of a window, what happens to him?
  c When S.H.I.E.L.D. wants Fury to destroy Manhattan with a nuclear weapon, what does he say?
  d When Loki says that Hulk can't hurt him, what does Hulk do?
  e When the nuclear weapon comes out of the top of the portal, what happens?
  f When Fury wants to use the Avengers again, will they come to him? What does he think?

Writing

19 Did you enjoy this story? Why (not)? Write about it.

20 Which Avenger would you like to be? Why? What did that Avenger do in this story?

21 You are Iron Man. Write about S.H.I.E.L.D.'s nuclear weapon. Why did they send it? What do you think about that? What did you do with the weapon? How did you feel?

22 You are one of the Avengers (but not Hulk). Why are you an Avenger? Why do you want to work with the other Avengers in the future? Write about your feelings.

23 You are Bruce Banner. Write a letter to Nick Fury after the story ends. What are you going to do now? Why do you not want to be an Avenger in the future?

24 Write a conversation between Thor and Loki after the story ends. They are back on Asgard. How does Thor feel about Loki? What does he want Loki to do? How does Loki feel about Thor? What is he going to do?

25 You are Fury. You work for S.H.I.E.L.D., but you are angry with them. Write to them. Tell them why.

26 Where are the Avengers going to go now? What are they going to do? We don't know, but what do you think? Write one or two sentences about each of them. Start: I think that ...

Word List

agent (n) James Bond is a British *agent* in books and movies. He works for the *agency* MI6.

armor (n) When fighters wore *armor* over their clothes, they didn't get hurt.

attack (n/v) After the *attack* in a busy street, ten people were dead.

avenge (v) He *avenged* the killing of his father; now the killer is dead.

bow and arrow (n phr) In the days before guns, people in many countries killed people and animals with *bows and arrows*.

destroy (v) Fire can *destroy* a house in minutes.

energy (n) He doesn't eat breakfast, so he has no *energy* in the morning.

explode (v) When the plane hit the ground, it *exploded*. We heard the *explosion* from a long way away.

hammer (n) Hit the glass with a *hammer* and the glass will break.

missile (n) When the *missile* hit the street, every building fell.

nuclear (adj) a kind of very *powerful energy*. A *nuclear weapon* can *destroy* a city.

portal (n) We went through the *portal*, into another world.

power (n) I can't drive fast. This car doesn't have much *power*. It isn't very *powerful*.

protect (v) I had to *protect* the children from a dangerous dog.

save (v) She jumped into the river and *saved* my life. I was *safe*.

scepter (n) In the picture Elizabeth II is wearing beautiful clothes and has a *scepter* in her hand.

shield (n) Carry your *shield* in front of you. Then people can't hurt you.

space (n) Yuri Gagarin, a Russian, was the first person in *space*. He flew around the Earth in a Vostok *spaceship*.

touch (v) Please don't *touch* the food with your dirty hands.

weapon (n) You can't carry guns or other *weapons* onto airplanes.